DR PHIL CUMMINS
CHARACTER EDUCATION SERIES

A Life of Purpose

A Life of
Purpose

DR PHIL CUMMINS
CHARACTER EDUCATION SERIES

A Life of
Purpose

For the architects of my life.

Published in 2025 by Amba Press, Melbourne, Australia
www.ambapress.com.au

© Phil Cummins 2025

All rights reserved. No part of this book may be reproduced or transmitted in any form or by any means, electronic or mechanical, including photocopying, recording or by any information storage and retrieval system, without prior permission in writing from the publisher.

Cover design: Tess McCabe
Internal design: Amba Press
Editor: Rica Dearman

ISBN: 9781923215740 (pbk)
ISBN: 9781923215757 (ebk)

A catalogue record for this book is available from the National Library of Australia.

Contents

Foreword ix
Introduction: A Life of Purpose 1

Chapter 1
Explore 3

Live with purpose 6
Become your best self 8
Do what really matters 10
Know what motivates you 13
Connect with your people and your place 16
Step Forward and Up: Explore 19

Chapter 2
Discover 21

Choose the right purpose 24
Build your character 26
Learn, live, lead and work well 29
Keep writing your story 31
See what lies beyond you 34
Step Forward and Up: Discover 37

Chapter 3
Encounter   39

Aim high   42
Measure yourself and your impact   46
Put others first   48
Be kind   51
Start with belonging   54
Step Forward and Up: Encounter   58

Conclusion: Let's go!   61

Foreword

Hi! My name is Phil.

For more than thirty-five years, as an educator, researcher and speaker, I've been talking with and listening to hundreds of thousands of students, their families and teachers all over the world as they tell me what they want for their lives.

My son, Oliver, would say that you need to be kind as you go about trying to build a good life. How about you? What would you say? What is your voice? How do you put this into practice in your agency? Who do you advocate for? How will you know you are pursuing a life that is both well-lived and worthwhile?

I think there are four ways you can grow in the character, competency and wellness you need for such a life:

1. **A Life of Purpose** – how to identify and claim the fundamental reason why for your journey of exploration, discovery and encounter.
2. **The Pathway to Excellence** – how to learn, live, lead and work as you strive to become the best version of yourself.
3. **Leading for Tomorrow's World** – how to connect your purpose to leadership which influences, inspires, directs and motivates others to build a shared vision for the future.

4. **Make a Difference** – how to create a plan to put your sense of purpose into practice for the sake of people and place and planet.

Drawing on the global research of three organisations that I lead (CIRCLE Education, a School for tomorrow. and the *Game Changers* podcast), I've written four books that explore in turn each of these four ways to grow in character. They're all about helping you to be well and grow in the knowledge, skills, dispositions and habits you need to understand what your purpose is and how you might learn, live, lead and work in pursuit of it.

This book, *A Life of Purpose*, is about the adventure of becoming *you*. It takes you through the stages of a journey in which you uncover the powerful rationale that will help you to weave together all the parts of your life to tell a story about yourself and your commitment to people and place and planet.

So, what do you want for your life? What's important to you? What will help you to make your mark and measure up? Are you ready to take the big Step Forward and Up through **A Life of Purpose**?

Let's go!

Phil

Dr Phil Cummins FRSA FACEL FIML
Managing Partner, a School for tomorrow.
Managing Director, CIRCLE – The Centre for Innovation,
 Research, Creativity and Leadership in Education
Associate Professor of Education and Enterprise
Honorary Senior Fellow, University of Melbourne
Host, *Game Changers* podcast

Introduction
A Life of Purpose

What is it that will make a difference in your life? What is it that will help you to connect with something bigger, something that goes beyond your own emotional, intellectual and physical self? What will help you to create a life that is both well-lived and worthwhile?

Young people all across the world tell me how they want to grow, make progress and achieve their goals. They want to feel successful and to enjoy their life in the process.

Most importantly, they also want to go beyond themselves, to be part of a community. They also tell me they want to connect with something that goes beyond their own emotional, intellectual and physical selves. They want to embark on a journey of exploration, discovery and encounter that takes them beyond self-interest towards selflessness. They recognise that to become the best version of themselves, they need to commit to their service of others. In doing so, they want to make a difference for the better – for their friends, family and even the world as a whole.

It's all about a life of purpose.

What does it mean to have 'a life of purpose'? It's about finding your compelling reason 'why?', a rationale for what it is that you want to do with your life, and then applying it to as much of what you do in your life as you can in ways that are:

- Meaningful – for good
- Authentic – for real
- Transformational – for change
- Sustainable – for life
- Selfless – for others
- Relational – for each other

You don't need to have the same sense of purpose forever. It can and will adapt as you change in how you want to live your life, the ways in which you connect with those around you, and as you learn to contribute in different ways to your community. Your fundamental purpose, therefore, is unlikely to change often; it will correspond to the steps you take towards the major milestones in your life. What is important, however, is that you do what you can to find a purpose that will carry you forward as you ask and answer questions about what really matters.

I want to help equip you with the curiosity, compassion, courage and conviction to keep going with finding your compelling reason 'why?', and not give up on making it happen. I want to empower you to strive to belong, to achieve your potential, and to do good and right. I want to enable you to adapt and organise yourself to meet the challenges and opportunities of the world around you with a sense of purpose that is shaped by your inner drive and the influence it has on others' lives, as well as your capacity to meet the reasonable expectations of others.

That's the character of **A Life of Purpose**.

Let's go!

Chapter 1
Explore

Explore

In this first chapter, I'd like to help you to explore what it means to live with purpose.

What does it feel like when you explore something or somewhere new? There's always a sense of excitement and wonder about the unknown. There's also a need to think through the steps you might take and how you can connect the different parts of your adventure, although you can't know everything in advance. You'll need to respond to and make decisions about what you find along the way. That's all part of the journey!

There are five key ideas in this chapter that will help you explore:

1. Live with purpose
2. Become your best self
3. Do what really matters
4. Know what motivates you
5. Connect with your people and your place

Let's work through each in turn.

You will then have an opportunity at the end of the chapter to Step Forward and Up by thinking about how you can connect with all five of these ideas on your own journey of exploration.

Live with purpose

What drives you forward in your life? What connects you to a sense of your potential to contribute to the broader world? What is your compelling reason 'why?'

It's all about **A Life of Purpose**. It's about claiming a fundamental reason for everything that you do in your life, and then going out and doing it.

I think that this is what a good life is really about; it's as much (if not more) about the others around you as it is yourself. The key assumption that underpins this is that a life of giving to others is transformative for each of us because it is grounded in the genuine meaningfulness that equips, empowers and enables us to make a difference.

As you do it, you need to ground this purpose in a practical understanding of what is important for you. My father, Brian, taught me about the value of doing the right thing. I think what he meant by this is that whatever you think you are meant to do, you have to be at ease with what and how you do this. Your purpose, therefore, needs to align with what you believe is good and right for you and for those around you.

Discovering what this purpose might be and how you might learn, live, lead and work well in pursuit of it requires you to embark on a personal journey of exploration, discovery and encounter towards character, competency and wellness.

Along the way, you will build your character.

Character is the way you live your life. Do you belong? Are you fulfilling your potential? Are you doing what is good and right?

These are powerful questions you can ask about your civic, performance and moral character. Sometimes to answer them you will search deep and discover an inner sense of who you are, and who you may become; this is your mark as a person. At other times, you try to fulfil the expectations of others; this is your measure as a person.

And so, through the course of your life, as you try to express the civic character of belonging, the performance character of fulfilling potential and the moral character of doing what is good and right, you will wrestle. You will wrestle with both leaving a mark and measuring up. This is how you form character. This is how you can show who you have been, and who you are becoming.

I'm not sure that anyone really has 'the answer' to everything. Nothing is that clear or certain, and there's never a one-size-fits-all solution. What I've learned from the stories of so many people around the world is that we are more likely to find the right way forward when we keep wrestling with the things that challenge, inspire and support us to move from who we were yesterday to who we are now towards who we might become tomorrow: a person of character, a person of purpose.

How will you demonstrate the character that allows you to live a life of purpose? You will reveal this through your competencies. What do I mean by this? A competency is the capacity to demonstrate how you have grown in character. It deliberately and simultaneously asks you to know, do, be and learn. When you master a competency, the knowledge, skills, dispositions and learning habits that are cultivated by the values that you have formed and the social and educational processes you have experienced will be demonstrated in the outcomes you demonstrate.

And you will build all of this on a foundation of your physical, psychological, emotional, intellectual and spiritual wellness.

If all things are as they ought to be, those strengths will have come to the fore and allow you to both leave your mark and to measure up in your community. You will connect to your people and your place and your planet to develop a sense of what really matters to you, and how this might be honoured through your practice.

You will live with purpose and become your best self.

> **Reflection: Live with purpose**
>
> What stands out with your character, your competency and your wellness?
>
> What are your strengths?
>
> What might become new strengths?

Become your best self

What might **A Life of Purpose** do for you?

How might your life of purpose take you beyond your own self?

How might you gain that deep experience of satisfaction, enjoyed by purpose-driven people all over the world, regardless of the challenges and opportunities that life presents?

When you commit to leading a life of purpose, you engage in a lifelong process of becoming a better version of yourself. With every step you take in **A Life of Purpose**, you will increasingly show what feels like the character, competency and wellness of which you are really capable.

In doing so, you will increasingly feel a sense of belonging, achieve your potential, and do what is good and right in your life.

When I've talked with people around the world about how they develop character, I've learned that if you feel as though you belong, you will be more likely to achieve your potential. If you feel as though you belong and are achieving your potential, then you will be more likely to do that which you believe is good and right in the world.

You will need, therefore, to choose and claim your purpose carefully and wisely.

And, of course, this is not about a selfish pursuit for personal gain. The value we create for ourselves is amplified when it is shared with generosity of spirit among others.

People are social beings and are meant to live in a community. Our weaknesses are, more often than not, compensated for by the strengths of others. In turn, our gifts find their truest and fullest expression when they serve the needs of others. There is a reciprocity, a mutual exchange of benefit about this which is very powerful.

We thrive best when we grow in our capacity to place the benefits of how we learn, live, lead and work for the benefit of others just as much as, if not more than, for ourselves. In other words, we thrive best individually and collectively when we are selfless.

When you commit to the process of identifying why you want to live your life and how you might put this into practice, it will be helpful for you to think about how best to place the needs of your people and place and planet first.

This is never an easy or simple thing to do. Life is complicated and never quite happens the way we might want. We can't control most, if not anything, in it. What we can do is to choose what will guide us to make the decisions about what we will and will not do.

Not everything is possible and not everyone can be a part of what we are trying to do. My friend Leann, a senior First Nations Bidjara/KaraKara woman who also acknowledges her South Sea Islander heritage, would say that we also need to think about who we will take with us and who we will leave behind on each stage of the journey. This doesn't mean that we don't care for and love those who will not be coming with us. It's just not their time to join up their songline with ours.

Thus, when you commit to putting your purpose into practice, you need to take responsibility for others, those who share a sense of, and find worth in, your purpose. By doing the things that matter most, you can become who you need to be as an individual for the sake of your people and your place and your planet. That's the true value of a life that's both well-lived and worthwhile – **A Life of Purpose**.

> ### Reflection: Become Your Best Self
>
> Can you identify a time when helping someone else made you feel good about yourself?
>
> Did you try to replicate that feeling through serving others on a different occasion?

Do what really matters

What do you really value in life? What is important to you? What are those powerful beliefs about what is good and right that guide you?

When you begin to contemplate what your purpose might be, it is helpful to contemplate both what is most true and relevant for your life – what really matters. You will need to identify those beliefs about what is good and right that can help you to identify and live with a purpose informed by values.

Sometimes, young people ask me about my own values. What matters to me? Over many years, I have drawn together a set of ideas that seem to bring direction and value to those I love and myself, especially in my work as a leader. I introduced them to you at the start of this book:

- Meaningfulness – for good
- Authenticity – for real
- Transformation – for change
- Sustainability – for life
- Selflessness – for others
- Relationship – for each other

You'll notice that I have framed each of my values as both a thing that I try to do and a reason for me doing it. That works well for me because it helps me to direct my intentions into actions.

You should, and will, have your own way of thinking about, identifying and expressing your values.

It's important to write these ideas down. If something is not written down, then it's most likely not real for you.

When you write your values down, you need to give power to these ideas by using them in everyday conversation. In particular, you need to make clear to those around you why you think that these values are the basis of what you think is good and right.

When you start to say your values out loud and use them in your daily conversations, you may feel a little awkward at first, but that's just a matter of practice. What's most relevant about this is that in saying what you believe is good and right in your world, you are committing to yourself and those around you to act in accordance with what you believe. This quality of integrity is valued highly; it allows you to be seen as a person of honour, as someone who keeps their word.

This may, in turn, cause you to feel uncomfortable when you don't act as you should. You won't be perfect in living out your values – but then, none of us is. What we can do is to be the best version of ourselves today and to find ways to improve what we do and become tomorrow.

In striving for improvement in executing your purpose in this way, you may never get as far or as deep as you might like in the things you do, but by focusing on doing what really matters to have an impact on your life and the lives of others, you will be transforming yourself and those around you. More and more, you will be doing those things that you believe are good and right.

In this way, leading **A Life of Purpose** means you are motivated to do the things that really matter – they're your most powerful reasons why.

Reflection: Do What Really Matters

What are your values?

What are the ideas and things that are really important to you?

Know what motivates you

How can you move from being engaged to feeling truly empowered to carry out your purpose in your world? What drives you to grow and learn? What is it that will motivate you to become the best version of yourself?

Perhaps no single phenomenon reflects the positive potential of human nature so much as motivation – the powerful reasons that lie behind what you do.

If you are driven solely by the extrinsic motivation that comes from pleasing or meeting the expectations of other people, you will always feel a certain kind of pressure to behave in a way that doesn't feel entirely like yourself; you will experience little to no autonomy. It can be useful for you to accept the structure of an externally imposed expectation, especially when you are learning how to do something for the first time. It can be hard to make things happen all by yourself.

On the other hand, when you are driven by intrinsic motivation, a deep inner drive, you feel self-directed and self-aware; you are more likely in the long run to feel the mastery, autonomy and purpose that will connect you to your preferred future.

I know that I'm motivated by a few things. I love a win and I love to see a plan come together. I love to see those around me whom I love grow and succeed. But I also love to know that I've played a part in this, that I've been helpful. Oliver would say that this is how your inner motivation can connect with your outer motivation – if you allow what's outside you to influence what emerges from your inner self. When your drive to become the best version of your inner self is connected to the wellbeing of those around you, then you can have a very powerful reason to do what you do, and the impact can be profound. Everyone can get a win!

But what about you? What motivates you?

What about happiness? Is it important to be happy? What role should happiness play in what motivates your sense of purpose?

A state of happiness is wonderful in the moment, but it can be occasional and fleeting. None of us can be happy all of the time; it's unrealistic to aim for this and it can set you up for disappointment. On the other hand, it's also damaging to deny yourself the chance of happiness because you're worried it might never happen. You have to have faith in the possibility that good and right things can and should happen to you at least some of the time.

We can all aspire to live with happiness in the knowledge that what endures and is most powerful in helping us to feel happy (more often than not) is the accomplishment of our purpose. This brings with it the joy that comes from realising the value and values that a life of purpose can bring to you and the people you love.

I've learned that lasting motivation can be sourced more often from the inner satisfaction that comes from the kindnesses you exchange, the gifts you provide and receive, and the legacy that you leave in pursuit of your purpose, rather than a desire to create your own short-term gratification. Indeed, many scholars will tell you that this capacity to delay your own self-gratification through regulating yourself is perhaps the most important character trait of all. You can't and shouldn't do it forever, but a healthy degree of self-discipline will go a very long way.

I've known my friend Chris for many years; we used to be roommates in boarding school and our lives have remained connected ever since. As a doctor, he's deeply committed to the wellness of his patients and to the sharing of knowledge in his profession. He gives much of his time to teach others how to do what he's learned about his speciality. He cares deeply for his family. His strong sense of self-discipline to put others first and the fundamental decency with which he does this drive him forward in all that he does. Chris inspires me greatly.

Ultimately, therefore, the quality of your contributions in **A Life of Purpose** can be seen in the positive impact you have on others. In other words, if your values and beliefs are being carried out faithfully through your actions, you will be revealing the sincerity of the purpose for which you really stand and how this might be dedicated to the people around you and the place that you call home.

> **REFLECTION: KNOW WHAT MOTIVATES YOU**
>
> Can you identify what drives you most to do the things you want to do?
>
> What about the things you need to do?
>
> What motivates you to hold to your purpose and get done the things that need to get done?

Connect with your people and your place

Who are your people and where is your place? How will you find them? How will you know when they are right for you?

We have already seen that **A Life of Purpose** is lived in community with others.

I've spent most of my life trying to work out where I feel as though I'm at home. Having lived in quite a few places as I grew up with my parents and then raised my own family, I'm lucky to have settled in recent years in the suburb of Fitzroy on Wurundjeri Woiwurrung country in Melbourne, Australia. It's where I feel as though I belong.

I travel around the world helping people and schools create the possibility of better outcomes for learners everywhere. I'm very blessed to have made many enduring connections with friends, family and colleagues in so many different communities. But I know where my home is. My place grounds me.

You need to be connected to the people with whom and the place where you feel as though you belong. Your personal journey of exploration, discovery and encounter towards character, competency and wellness requires you from the outset to contemplate the significance of a shared humanity in situ, rather than just the attainment of your individual desires and needs.

I believe that your understanding of the world around you and what you might do with this world is infinitely improved when you accept that you simply cannot do it all yourself. You alone do not have the power to affect all of the change that you need or wish to occur. You must rely on those around you for challenge, inspiration and support. For those of you with a specific faith, you will most likely rely on your understanding of God most of all to show you the way.

This purpose-driven connection with others will not necessarily be automatic. There must be a fair exchange of value between you for it to work out for the sake of all. You will need to weigh up the benefits that you can give and receive in turn from your people and place, and perhaps even change them over time as the cycles of your life change. This requires of you a reciprocity that comes from the transference of benefit. I think of it in this way: I am because you give.

The shared culture of your community and the collective discipline that exists within it to help its members to inspire, support and challenge each other towards a life of purpose is cultivated by habits of trust, responsibility and self-discipline.

For me, it's been so valuable to have had a small group of friends who I have known for more than 40 years now who have done so much to shape my understanding of people and place. My long-standing friend Georgina, in particular, inspires me with her lifelong pursuit of her professional accomplishment, her education and the best interests of her family. She has a clear sense of what matters to her and uses it to make the easy and difficult daily decisions that come with adult life. This is deeply wrapped up in her sense of her people and her place. She also keeps me honest when I think just a little too much about myself and lose touch with the experiences that have shaped my own people and place.

It is this combination of culture and cultivation that will enable you to make the right choice for deciding what is your own purpose.

Reflection: Connect with your people and your place

Who are your people?

How do they help you to become the best version of yourself?

Where is your place?

How does being connected to your place help you feel as though you belong?

Step Forward and Up

Explore

We've come to the end of the first chapter of **A Life of Purpose**. You've had the opportunity to think through and reflect on five key ideas:

- ✓ Live with purpose
- ✓ Become your best self
- ✓ Do what really matters
- ✓ Know what motivates you
- ✓ Connect with your people and your place

At the end of each chapter, I'd like you to take the key ideas and think about how you'd like to step forward and up with them. In this first Step Forward and Up, in particular, I'd like you to think through two important questions about how to connect with these five ideas as you take your own journey of exploration:

1. What opportunities does your world offer you?
2. What do you have to offer your world?

Finally, based on everything you have thought about over the course of this chapter, we are going to help you to build a plan to Step Forward and Up. We are going to use the Plus, Minus, Interesting process first developed by Dr Edward de Bono, and it's important for you to write down your answers to each of these:

- **Plus** – What's one idea from this chapter that you could make happen in your life tomorrow? What could you do to make this happen? What help will you need? What's a really practical first thing that you could do to make this idea real in your life? What will you do to keep going? How will you know when it's making a difference?

- **Minus** – What's one idea from this chapter that doesn't seem right for you? Why isn't this idea right for you? Is it a case of 'not at all' or 'not yet'? How do you know whether you should hold your ground or shift your thinking on this idea?

- **Interesting** – What's one idea from this chapter that seems like it might be an interesting thing to do but which you're not yet ready to embrace? What might you need to do to ready yourself for this challenge? Who or what might help you to prepare you to take up this challenge in due course? How will you allow the time and space to do this preparation?

Thank you for putting together your first plan. It may take some time to create habits and dispositions that will help you to feel that stepping forward and up is natural. That's OK – every change you make takes time to become truly part of the way you do things as you explore **A Life of Purpose**.

What does it mean, then, to explore **A Life of Purpose**? You will learn from others, learn with others, do it yourself and share with others. You will connect with people and place and planet to develop a sense of your purpose and how this might be brought to life in your practice. You will build the character that allows you to feel a sense of belonging, fulfil your potential and do some good and right in the world. At the same time, if you grow in your competency and nurture your wellness, and if at least most things are as they ought to be, your strengths will have come to the fore. You will be able to make your mark and measure up. You will begin to live **A Life of Purpose**.

When you are ready, let's start Chapter 2 in which you will move into the second stage of **A Life of Purpose**: discovery.

Let's go!

Chapter 2
Discover

Discover

In this second chapter of **A Life of Purpose**, we will consider how to discover and choose the right purpose.

How does it feel when you discover something new for the first time? Do you feel excited? Nervous? Curious? As you start to contemplate the different possibilities that might be presented to you by your discovery, you'll see things you haven't come across before. You'll begin to think ahead about what might come next and how you might get there. You'll also want to stay in the moment and enjoy what is right in front of you.

There are five key ideas that will help you with discovery:

1. Choose the right purpose
2. Build your character
3. Learn, live, lead and work well
4. Keep writing your story
5. See what lies beyond you

We can work through these together and then think about how they can come together to support you in the moment of discovery in the second Step Forward and Up.

Choose the right purpose

What possible purpose could you choose? How might you respond to the challenges and opportunities presented by others while also taking responsibility for your own inner sense of what you might be doing? How can you develop a solution for your purpose which feels right for you, a 'best fit' that will serve you well, even if it is a compromise of what might be a 'perfect fit'?

Locating a purpose for the next stage of your life will start with developing an understanding of both the value you place on yourself and others, the things in which you are engaged, and also the values you hold that will tell you that these are the right things to do.

This process will be influenced strongly by your inner drive. It will be both bound and enhanced by that community which comprises your people and your place. It will also be directed by your honesty with yourself about what matters less and the opportunities that you do not wish to take up at this stage.

Thus, your emerging sense of purpose will also arise from a set of beliefs and perceptions about yourself that includes:

- Your sense of who you are, who you are becoming and how you relate to others
- Your attitude and how it affects your self-awareness, interest, relevance and curiosity
- Your adaptive expertise and self-efficacy. Adaptive expertise means how you build and use your character and competencies to solve known and new problems; it is, in essence, your commitment to growth. Self-efficacy means how you set goals, organise yourself and the way you learn, live, lead and work to optimise your character and competencies so that you can thrive in your world; it is your capacity to determine the course of your life

There is so much to do in life and so many options of pathways that you can follow. I'm convinced that you don't have to know your 'forever' purpose to lead a life of purpose. Sometimes you just need clarity around what comes next so you can direct your attention to it with energy, enthusiasm and focus.

Sometimes a process of elimination can be helpful to give you a set of choices that might help you refine your possible choices down to some realistic options. One way to do this is to work out the pathways that you do not wish to take and the people you would prefer not to join you on your journey at this stage.

On other occasions, it will be more straightforward – a matter of choosing from a few clear options that present themselves. You can also take the time to try out one of these potential pathways for a short while, especially when you are not sure that it is the best one for you. From there, you can begin to develop a sense of what a 'best fit' might be and map the best way forward for you.

Perhaps it's a matter of asking the right questions. I believe that as we ask and answer fundamental questions that connect us to our purpose, we build the adaptive expertise and self-efficacy to build character and experience success in how we learn, live, lead and work on our journey of exploration, discovery and encounter that is **A Life of Purpose**.

Once you become motivated to achieve, you will eventually exert your effort, time and energy towards becoming better at becoming a better version of yourself. This is called self-actualising. You will begin to self-actualise because you make the right choices and carry them out. This is called self-determination, and it is the most powerful force you will encounter in choosing your purpose and shaping your character.

My friend and colleague David has taught generations of students the value of History; he taught me many years ago and since then we have worked together, written books and enjoyed sharing each other's company. Throughout his life, he's retained his curiosity. He's always asking really good questions about people and place and planet. He's also blessed with a strong need to get a move-on! He's a great example of how energy and inquiry can act on each other to fuel the way forward in a life of learning, character and contribution.

> **Reflection: Choose the right purpose**
>
> What are you most curious to learn about in life?
>
> What feels like the best use of your time?
>
> What motivates you to do more in certain areas?
>
> What gives you the most satisfaction – what do you most enjoy doing?
>
> What helps you to feel as though you are becoming the best version of yourself?

Build your character

Do you **belong**? Are you **fulfilling your potential**? Are you doing what is **good and right**?

I introduced you to these questions in Chapter 1. You can use them to help you track how you are building:

- The **civic character of belonging** that is typically described through qualities such as **courtesy**, **consideration for others** and **respect**

- The **performance character of fulfilling potential** that people often associate with qualities of **purpose**, **persistence** and **reflection**
- The **moral character of doing good and right** that is consistently connected with **courage**, **honesty** and **humility**

More broadly, you build your character in how you live your life; it's how you apply your adaptive expertise and self-efficacy to live out your purpose and thrive in your world. You develop it through both the inner drive to realise your own sense of who you might become, as well as by responding to the replication of external standards that others set for you.

If you have been honest with yourself, you will have seen that your character will be worked on and revealed in good times and bad, in moments of both mundanity and great excitement. It will be more than just one thing, or the thing that happens when no one is around. It will be the integrated product of your knowledge, skills, dispositions and habits of mind, all of which should be directed concurrently towards a quest to go from the dislocation of self-centredness to the integrity and wholeness of a selfless person who leaves a mark and meets the measure of the world through the pursuit of the right purpose.

We live in a rapidly changing world. Everyday life means living through complexity, being ready for the things that life throws at us and enjoying the good fortune with which we are blessed. There is a volume, pace and intensity to our times that mean we need to be in a position to respond to change readily and willingly. This means that all of us need to be able to meet these challenges and to make the most of the opportunities that are presented to us.

In practical terms, how people see and assess your character will become the sum of the competencies through which you will enact your purpose. My friend Julie is a terrific example of this. She's determined and fierce-willed about creating the best possible opportunities for young people to thrive because they know who they are and how to draw on the reserves of their character to serve their community. Her life is a case study in how to build your own character through helping others to build theirs.

In this way, your character is the work of a lifetime in the world. It will tell the story of your yesterday, your today and your tomorrow.

Your story will emerge from the formation of your identity throughout this narrative and the accumulation of your impact on the lives of others and the environment around you. It will be the by-product of your commitment to seek out the best version of yourself and, although never perfect or complete, it can be capable of achieving significance and goodness (or otherwise, depending on your values and how you enact them).

> ### Reflection: Build Your Character
>
> What words do others use to describe your character?
>
> How would you describe your own character?
>
> What do you do to build your character?
>
> What do you do to test your character?
>
> How do you know when you act with good character?

Learn, live, lead and work well

What is it that you want to be good at doing? What are you already good at doing? What competencies do you want to improve and what are some that you don't yet have in your personal toolkit?

Mastering the competencies to learn, live, lead and work are ongoing challenges that speak to your formation as a person. This natural and normal process of asking questions that help to form and develop you as a person is called **The Pathway to Excellence**. We will explore this in depth in the next volume of this **Character Education Series**, but for now it's useful to introduce the idea to you here.

The competency you gain in answering the question 'who am I?' is the competency to learn. Learning well helps you to become stronger in all the facets of your life and apply these strengths to realising an evolving and increasingly selfless reason for doing what you do. Learning, therefore, is about the quest towards self-awareness that fosters a sense of your purpose through a combination of both curiosity and wisdom so that you can meet the expectation to 'know yourself'.

The competency gained in answering the question 'where do I fit in?' is the competency to live. Living well helps you to understand and respect yourself and others, and the language, customs, honourable traditions, rituals and values of the people and places from which you have come and to where you are going. Living, therefore, is the search for relationship that helps you to appreciate your people and your place with the humility and gratitude that help you to meet the expectation to 'earn your place'.

The competency gained from answering the question 'how can I best serve others?' is the competency to lead. Leading well begins with who you are, flows into who you want to become and is demonstrated through deliberate, targeted and intentional action that aligns vision with intention and means to direct, motivate, influence and inspire others to achieve a preferred future for all. Leading, therefore, is about the challenge of selflessness that helps you to locate your practice with the courage and compassion necessary to meet the expectation to 'go on a journey from me to you to us'.

The competency gained from answering the question 'whose am I?' is the competency to work. Working well is about building around you a supportive network of people for and with whom your sense of belonging, the achievement of your potential, and the propensity to do that which is good and right in your life – your character – might find a meaningful home. Working, therefore, is about the discovery of commitment that helps you to connect your purpose, your people and your place within your practice through the vocation and diligence required to meet the expectation to 'find your calling'.

What do I mean by a calling or a 'vocation'?

Our life's journey asks each of us to grow in our capacity to ask and answer these four questions and reflect upon our purpose, our 'why?'. Why do you do what you do? Why are you who you are? Who and what might be the proper objects of such a purpose? How do you and will you act on this? What will be your legacy?

A sense of vocation speaks to this overwhelming desire to ask and answer such questions. It asks you to name and claim a purpose in response to them as an essential part of the journey of a lifetime, no matter what it is you actually end up doing for work. Vocation connects how you work to how you learn, live and lead. In fact, a vocation is a calling to do work for the sake of others – for people and place and planet. It's in contemplation of the other that we locate purpose and put it into practice in the stories of our lives.

On our separate and connected journeys, each of us needs to grow in our vocation as much as we do in all the other parts of our lives.

In the hustle and bustle of daily life, it can be easy for us to give all our energy and effort to that which lies immediately in front of us. Yet, the urgent demands of today can take precedence over the equally important need to tend to the garden of tomorrow if we don't take the time to reflect and plan our way forward.

You can and will do none of these competencies of learn, live, lead and work completely or separately. Each of us has strengths and weaknesses, and the way we cope with the vicissitudes of life is never as constant as we would wish. You will surprise yourself on occasion, just as much as you will disappoint yourself. It's all part of your story, and so much of that is influenced by the questions you can ask to guide your process of inquiry.

> ### Reflection: Learn, live, lead and work well
>
> Learning is about self-awareness, living is about relationship, leading is about selflessness and working is about vocation – all of us will benefit from mastery of each of these capacities.
>
> Is there anything that is holding you back from growing in each of these capacities?
>
> What questions might you ask that will help you find a way forward?

Keep writing your story

Where have you come from, where are you now and where are you going? Can you create a story that allows you to continue to become the person you should be? How might you share this story with others?

People grow and change throughout their lives. They do both right and wrong things in the natural course of events that intersect with where they have been, where they are now and where they are going. People have been telling stories of this for as long as they have gathered together. It's humanity's oldest and most powerful form of how we connect people to place and (ultimately) purpose. It is as much a narrative of journey as it is a description of destination.

Can I share with you some of my story?

I'm Phil – more formally, Dr Philip Sebastian Antony Cummins. I was born and educated on Gadigal land in Sydney; I now live on Wurundjeri Woiwurrung country in the suburb of Fitzroy, Melbourne. I'm a loyal and critical Australian by birth, and I'm an educator by trade and conviction.

I began teaching History and Latin more than 30 years ago. Since then, I've worked in and with schools, travelling the world as a teacher, researcher, writer, leader and colleague, and a professor of education and enterprise. I'm a father to three grown-up children and I'm both Pa and Yeye to a grandson who's named after my father. I've worked for my local church and its community. I've served my country as a soldier. I've written a lot of books and articles – all up millions of words in history and education, particularly about the strategy, leadership, governance and culture that help to describe an authentic vision for learning and make real its power to transform the lives of students, their families and teachers through sustainable high performance in schools.

I owe a lot of all of this to my parents.

Dr Brian Patrick Cummins was an accomplished architect and artist, as well as a successful investor in small ventures. This shy and awkward man, to whom I'm still trying to prove myself even though he died of cancer in 2008, taught me three big lessons:

1. "Whatever happens in life, you have to sleep at night." That's the deep thinker and complicated but visionary moralist speaking.
2. "Everyone has to be able to feed their family." That's the public servant and family man talking.
3. The third lesson is from the world of cricket – his great love: "You have to get in behind the line of the ball."

My mum, Dr Rohma Newman Cummins (who's still going at 92) is a fierce and trailblazing pathologist, scientist, orchestra manager, gardener and educator. From her have come lessons about the primacy of the value of education in propelling a life forward, the importance of striving for both excellence and truth, and the finding of them in the details, and, most of all, the enduring need to hang on in hope, no matter the circumstances. Giving up is no valid option. You'd better do what you say you're going to do, and you'd better keep going till it's done!

A lot of what I learned from my parents matches what I've also learned from young people, their families, teachers and communities all over the world. Although each person is home to a unique life, we are all woven into the fabric of a common and interdependent humanity.

What about you, though? What is your story?

Your story is being created as you live it. Look around you. Gather the episodes, experiences and evidence of your growth. Then try to map out a version of it that you might find truthful and helpful in explaining how you have pursued your purpose.

Your story also needs to help people to see the tangible scale of your world so that they can walk in it alongside you with the confidence and safety that comes from knowing that you have their best interests at heart. To do this, you'll need to see beyond yourself to where the people in your life are, and then offer them a hand so that you can lead them towards a preferred future together.

> **REFLECTION: KEEP WRITING YOUR STORY**
>
> What is the best version of you?
>
> How have you learned to be like this?
>
> What have you done to be a role model for others?
>
> What might come next?

See what lies beyond you

Who am I? Where do I fit in? How can I best serve others? Whose am I?

These are the four questions that drive the development of the competencies to learn, live, lead and work that underpin all of the processes of **The Pathway to Excellence** to which I introduced you earlier in this chapter. Inherent within this process is a willingness to become a better version of yourself.

This desire to improve who you are is more than a commendable attitude; it's a necessary and normal part of **A Life of Purpose**. Regularly reflecting on and reviewing your own performance shows your commitment to growth, and to developing and mastering those habits required to be the best version of yourself that you can be today and to become a better version tomorrow.

What are these habits?

You need to know what you need to be learning – that's aspiration. You need to go on a journey of discovery, encounter, challenge and connection – that's experience. You need to collaborate with your teachers, mentors and experts as the co-authors of the narrative of your learning journey – that's agency. You need to discover your own identity and how best to express it through your learning and relationships – that's voice. And you need to organise yourself to have the time, support and conditions that will help you to make the most of your learning to make progress and achieve success – that's resource.

Yet, self-improvement is not enough to create a purpose sufficient enough to make your life whole. You will also need to confront the reality that you are not the centre of the universe and that you cannot live your life just pleasing yourself.

I'm convinced that in coming to accept and claim your purpose, you will need to acknowledge that doing something better with some sense of higher mission means seeing the reality that life is better for everyone when you consistently place the interests of others before your own.

My older son, James, is a fine example of the way in which you can balance being true to yourself while seeing what lies beyond you. He has his own way of doing things which he has learned over many years; his habits are integral to his values and the way he cares for people and relationships in his own family. He understands well the need to seek satisfaction through service, not by being someone other than himself, but by working hard towards becoming the best version of himself that he can possibly be at any given point in time.

In finding your sense of purpose in the truth that lies beyond you and your care for the other, you will learn much about the importance of obedience, humility and forbearance in your connections and relationships with others. You will realise that service means more than just doing nice things for other people to make yourself feel better about yourself or fulfilling the drive of a selfish gene that sees a benefit in the hope of the exchange of do-gooding.

> **Reflection: See What Lies Beyond You**
>
> What do you currently do for other people, both in small and great ways, for which you expect nothing in return?
>
> What more might you be doing and for whom?
>
> How might you do this without harming yourself and your own development?

Step Forward and Up
Discover

I believe that discovering the truth that lies beyond ourselves allows us to connect deeply to our sense of purpose. Your commitment to the situation of the other goes beyond feeling and knowing; it converts the motivations and actions of your labour and your being into a vocation – the attachment of your purpose to your inner drive so that how you learn, live, lead and work is articulated most fully and meaningfully in what you do for your people and your place.

Before we move on to the next stage of **A Life of Purpose**, let's review what we have learned in this second chapter about discovery. We have focused on five key ideas:

- ✓ Choose the right purpose
- ✓ Build your character
- ✓ Learn, live, lead and work well
- ✓ Keep writing your story
- ✓ See what lies beyond you

Think through each of these ideas again. Would you like to step forward and up with them? Start by completing the following statements:

> *What the world needs now is…*
>
> *What I can do about this is…*
>
> *What I can actually do to make a difference (no matter how small) in bringing this about is…*

Based on everything you have thought about over the course of this chapter, let's build a plan to Step Forward and Up. We are going to use Dr Edward de Bono's Plus, Minus, Interesting process again; it's still important for you to write down your answers to each of the stages of questioning:

- **Plus** – What's one idea from this chapter that you could make happen in your life tomorrow? What could you do to make this happen? What help will you need? What's a really practical first thing that you could do to make this idea real in your life? What will you do to keep going? How will you know when it's making a difference?

- **Minus** – What's one idea from this chapter that doesn't seem right for you? Why isn't this idea right for you? Is it a case of 'not at all' or 'not yet'? How do you know whether you should hold your ground or shift your thinking on this idea?

- **Interesting** – What's one idea from this chapter that seems like it might be an interesting thing to do but which you're not yet ready to embrace? What might you need to do to ready yourself for this challenge? Who or what might help you to prepare you to take up this challenge in due course? How will you allow the time and space to do this preparation?

It's also important to think about how what you decide fits in with the commitments you made to yourself at the end of Chapter 1. How are you going with them? Is there anything that needs revising? Is there anything that needs to be left behind now? How can you blend the two sets of commitments into one plan?

Take your time to think about how these layers of planning and personal development might work together. When you are ready, let's start Chapter 3: encounter.

Let's go!

Chapter 3
Encounter

Encounter

The final stage of **A Life of Purpose** is encounter.

As you go on your journey of exploration and discovery, who are the people you will meet along the way? Where will you go? In what condition will you leave the planet that we all share? Encounter is about how we interact with 'the other' – our people and place and planet – and the legacy that we will leave behind when we have completed our time together with them.

There are five key ideas that help to explain your interdependence with and impact on the world and all who dwell in it as you encounter this and them:

1. Aim high
2. Measure yourself and your impact
3. Put others first
4. Be kind
5. Start with belonging

I'd like you to work through each in turn with me, then Step Forward and Up.

Aim high

What does it mean to make your mark? How would you know if you measure up? What might describe the quality of a life that's well-lived and worthwhile?

Questions such as these ask you to consider how your civic, performance and moral character interact with the lives of others. They require you to dig deep within yourself to find an inner sense of where you are in the story of who you have been, who you are and who you might become. This is called your personal 'mark'. You must also identify your 'measure', or how you are trying to live up to others' expectations. Developing your character in **A Life of Purpose** is about wrestling with both your mark and your measure. As you wrestle with yourself, your context and your capacity to contribute to the best of your ability, you will grow in the civic character of belonging, the performance character of realising your potential, and the moral character of doing what is good and right.

I believe that the journey of learning towards character needs to connect us to the essential questions that we all have and point us towards a way to find answers to them. The power of this inquiry to help us all to live better lives, to help us feel as though we are making a difference in the world, to help us to know that we are getting somewhere, must be sourced in the message we use to talk about it. It must be so significant, so rich and perhaps even so disruptive of our frame of mind that it compels us to sit up and take notice. It must force us to want to do something about it. It must make us commit to aiming high and finding our way in **A Life of Purpose**.

Aiming high, therefore, is about knowing who you want to become and how that will bring tangible benefit to the lives of those whom you encounter along the way. You will know you are doing this because you will begin to achieve one or more of six outcomes of thriving that the CIRCLE Education team has identified in our research work with people and communities all over the world.

Thriving means how people become the best versions of themselves. Their lives are well-lived and worthwhile not just because they achieve their goals, but also as much for the way in which they:

- Have the integrity and character to lead meaningful lives as **good people**
- Handle complex situations with authenticity as **future builders**
- Grow and transform as **continuous learners and unlearners**
- Guide society in a more sustainable direction as **solution architects**
- Balance local, regional and global perspectives selflessly as **responsible citizens**
- Work well with others to achieve success and fulfilment as relational **team creators**

Let's consider each of these outcomes in turn.

Good people want to be people of good character. They are committed to becoming virtuous. They have a coherent set of values and beliefs that guide them to do the right thing and to live a good life as best as they can. None of us is perfect, particularly when it comes to putting into place difficult values like honesty, responsibility and courage. But good people demonstrate their commitment enough to show the character required to stand strong in the face of adversity and place the needs of others before self-interest.

Future builders want to be leaders for the future. Inspired by authenticity, they have the reflectiveness, sensitivity and strength to honour the legacy of yesterday, attend to the needs of today and look forward to what tomorrow will require of us. While many leaders only concentrate on the demands of the present, future builders dream of tomorrow. They use patience, judgement and insight to build the narrative that helps us to forge a path towards this preferred future and bring others on the journey. They justify what we need to do, and how and why we should do this. They seek to communicate effectively. This relies on the capacity to address different audiences and purposes with clear and accurate expression that is well-informed, reliable and persuasive.

Continuous learners and unlearners prepare for a lifetime of learning, including the unlearning and relearning that will be required along their journey. They are equipped to become dynamic learners who are committed to continuing growth and improvement throughout their lives. They use the power of harnessing their curiosity, resourcefulness and adaptability to help us to transform gracefully from who we are today towards becoming the people we need to be in the future. They embrace change in their lives. This relies on the capacity to take responsibility for learning from all situations with a willing, open and agile mind that can assemble and master a dynamic and volatile body of knowledge that is informed by past practice, current experience and the anticipation of future needs.

Solution architects aim to design and generate effective solutions to emerging problems and issues. Inspired by the intention of sustainability, they are equipped to provide direction supported by successful answers to the questions of a world that seeks clarity and certainty in circumstances that are rapidly evolving and multidimensional. They use grit, perseverance and attention to detail to give others the confidence to meet expectations by thinking through options, and constructing, testing, implementing and evaluating solutions to familiar and unfamiliar problems. They show others a better way forward by charting a course towards a better normal and a shared understanding of excellence. They think through problems with confidence. Not every solution will be new, but all solutions will be crafted from an abiding curiosity about the world and an inclination to simply try new things. They never want to stand still and accept the status quo as the inevitable model or process of doing things.

Responsible citizens are sincere and selfless contributors who are prepared to put the common interest and the needs of others before themselves. They are dedicated to serving others. They have a balanced perspective that is informed by their desire to create belonging, achieve potential, and do what is good and right. Responsible citizens recognise that the interconnected nature of our civilisation demands of us the capacity to find ways to honour their obligations, pursue their purpose and make these feelings operate at local, regional and global levels as best as they can, even when things can (and inevitably) go wrong. They contribute positively to their communities. They appreciate that citizenship competency involves balancing local, regional and global perspectives and intent through recognising, identifying with and contributing to different communities.

Team creators know how to build and work well within teams. Inspired by relationality, they have the ability to create human-centred collaboration meaningfully, compassionately and productively in ways that bring out the best outcomes for all. They are inspired to become honourable colleagues who recognise our common humanity and work to enhance it. They use respect, kindness and appreciation for individual enterprise and shared endeavour to give us the sense of team and generosity of spirit to conquer the sense of isolation and alienation that divides people and organisations. They engage and work with others towards a common good through the strength of their empathy and competency to listen. They work well with all people because they know representation matters.

You don't need to be all of these things at any given point in time. They're ideals that can serve to describe what you become. To make progress in **A Life of Purpose**, you don't have to be perfect or extraordinary to succeed. You simply must be committed to aim high, claim your purpose and pursue outcomes of thriving through a process of wrestling with your character, growing in your competency and building the wellness you need to become the best version of yourself.

> **Reflection: Aim High**
>
> Which of these outcomes best describes you now?
>
> Assuming you can't be all things to all people, who do you want to become?
>
> What might you do to encounter others in this way?

Measure yourself and your impact

How would you know that you are becoming the person you should be? What evidence could you use to evaluate your impact? How might this be tracked against your sense of purpose?

As your personal journey of exploration, discovery and encounter continues, you will grow in character, competency and wellness. You will make progress (on occasion) and achieve success in demonstrating your graduate outcomes. Improvement is likely to be incremental and will rarely move in a straight line.

My daughter, Harriet, is a person who is very diligent. She sets goals and works hard to achieve them. She makes decisions thoughtfully, always mindful that to get where she might go, she will need to take a risk that her chosen path may not be the right one. She has the courage to reflect on her own situation at a given point in time and ask searching questions: Is this the right thing to do? Is this the right thing for me? What opportunity would I give up to take this pathway? How might I choose a better path?

It's too easy for each of us to slide into the habit of not asking the difficult questions about our own progress and success. We need to build habits that help us to challenge our assumptions; a disposition towards growth-minded change is essential.

I believe that life is no rehearsal. It would be a shame to miss the chance to make the most of the opportunities that have been given to us to learn, live, lead and work during our time on this planet. We need to want to do something about this. We need to want to be there and to make that difference!

For you to know that you've improved and are making that difference, you'll need to gather some evidence about where you started and where you've reached so you'll know where you are on your journey. You'll also need to take the opportunity to measure and warrant your contributions in a way that allows you to demonstrate and claim your purpose as the most compelling reason for your story. You don't have to measure everything at once, but it will help if you think through how you are growing in character, competency and wellness to start.

While it's natural to compare how you are going relative to the journeys of other people, it's far more important to gain a sense of who you are and who you are becoming. What's most important is to measure yourself against your purpose and the impact it has on the lives of others.

> **Reflection: Measure yourself and your impact**
>
> What is it that you want to do for yourself and other people in your life?
>
> What are you getting done on a regular basis?
>
> What else might be done?

Put others first

Do you see the value, dignity and worth of other people? What value do you bring to their lives? Are you the servant of your fellows?

It's important in **A Life of Purpose** that you look after yourself, particularly your wellness and the growth in your character and competency. The development of self, however, is not simply a solo exercise; it is always truly grounded in the service of others and the choice to place their needs before your own. Doing good things for people invokes both an awareness of the self and the other.

The challenges and opportunities of our world require each of us to take long-term action as individuals striving towards a better future. At the same time, your sense of how to apply shared values, create culture and develop the right solutions should grow as you form connections and close friendships with people of your age and stage of development. Together, you will learn, interact and become increasingly responsible for your actions. This has to be done while you juggle your own daily tasks and needs (like your relationships and education) with the things that happen on a wider scale.

You need to be well to manage all of this with success. On your journey, you will be supported by your peers, family and mentors. You also need to take responsibility for your own wellness, which directly impacts your character, affecting how you live and who you become. You need to look after your physical, mental, emotional and spiritual health, as well as your life satisfaction and your connection to your community.

This connection will be grounded in the respect you have for those who have come before you, those who are presently living within your community and those who are yet to come. In time, this respect will also be given to you as you earn your place. The respect will become mutual, especially through the values that you share with each other.

Who do you have in your life who models respect for you? Think of a person who habitually thinks of the needs of others. They show certain qualities in how they attend to these needs, yet much of what they do is also about their capacity to observe and notice. They take the time to care for the other because they see the value in giving. Putting others first is inherent in the accomplishment of their purpose.

Perhaps the hardest aspect of this is to remember that it is in the act of listening that we can come to learn more about another than we can in expressing our own voice. That we find our own voice and have it respected and celebrated by others is essential to our own development. Yet, truly hearing what others say and feel in company will take us much further than speaking to an empty room.

The signals that we give when we allow the time and show the care required to hear what others say about their lives – their joys and sorrows, their hard work and frustrations – are indeed potent. They help us to demonstrate tangibly that the person in front of us matters and is worth our attention and consideration. We do not have to agree with everything they say or do. We just have to care and, in all likelihood, so long as there is mutual interest and cause, they will care enough also to want to pay us the same accord in their own way. If we both care enough and listen hard, we can find a shared narrative that will connect our two stories and, for a while at least, make them one. Together, we might find meaningful ways to work together to help each other, to face our difficulties, to achieve our goals and become the people we need to become while we enjoy each other's company and what we both bring to the team we have created.

Development and attainment of your purpose, therefore, goes beyond the simple acquisition of resources or status for yourself. You need to consider how you might act to better the condition of all – not just those whom you know and like, but all within your community and perhaps even beyond.

I believe that **A Life of Purpose** must, ultimately, be selfless for it to be both well-lived and worthwhile. In fact, often the best way to realise who we might become is through our love, care and dedication for the people in our lives. It is about becoming a servant for the other.

Some forbearance is essential in helping us to take the time needed to understand and appreciate where others are in their lives and what brought them there, as is a tendency towards humility, which allows us to see their needs as being more important than our own.

Being a servant of others, however, does not mean being a pushover. We can't allow ourselves to be used or exploited unfairly. We must be prepared to assert what we believe is good and right, so long as we nestle this within an approach to seek the best for others, especially in how we show kindness to their human condition as part of **A Life of Purpose**.

> **REFLECTION: PUT OTHERS FIRST**
>
> How do other people put you first in their lives?
>
> What might you learn from these examples?
>
> How might you become an example of putting others first?

Be kind

Who do you care for? Who do you love? How do you want to make a difference in the lives of others?

Making a difference – having the right impact – is something that can compel you to embark on and continue the journey of exploration, discovery and encounter. It can be a journey of character development that is focused on the needs of others as a vocation, a calling. It can encourage you to take on challenges and take up opportunities. As you step forward and up, you can come to realise that it's not just about you – it's about us and how we live together.

Yet, relationships are difficult to sustain. We need people to connect with us and connect us to others and help to build a common culture of values, beliefs, goals, processes and norms of behaviour – the way we do things here. These need to include helping us all to reflect on ourselves individually and collectively so that we can celebrate our wins, develop our strengths and resolve any conflicts or uncertainties that arise. We also need people to help us to sharpen our individual self-efficacy – how we organise ourselves so that we put our character, competencies and wellness to their best use – and turn them into collective efficacy – how we organise a group of people into a team who are working together to achieve a common mission that fulfils the needs of the community which they serve, the team itself and the individuals within it.

This means we need people who can draw the best out of us. We need people who can help us to grow in character, to help us feel as though we belong, that we are fulfilling our potential, and we are doing what is good and right in the world. This means we need people who we feel are on our side and who understand what we are going through. This quality of empathy goes beyond feeling sorry for someone. There needs to be a genuine desire to create solutions that can nurture, challenge and inspire us to grow in our character, competencies and wellness.

We also need people to grow us in our adaptive expertise so that our competencies can be put to the best possible use in new situations. In this way, we need to be supported to respond to change constructively, even when we find such change personally and professionally difficult.

As we work on the hard things in **A Life of Purpose** together, we can see that growth, character and purpose are all about the wrestling – the wrestling between where we were yesterday, where we are today and where we might be tomorrow. It's about our mark as a person (who we feel we might become from the inside) and our measure as a person (how we respond to external expectations). Yet we can't resolve this on our own and what resolution we achieve is flawed. No solution ever comes close to our dreams.

I believe that there is no self-help regime that can provide quick solutions or perfect answers to difficult situations. Life is neither quick nor perfect. Instead, it's a lot of hard work over a long time. That's how you move forward in **A Life of Purpose**. That's why, as we say in our family, 'hard is good'.

Most people are able to tell you important stories of how they grew in character because of their capacity to make it through tough times. Many people believe that the character we acquire in times of adversity is, in fact, truer than other types of character. I'm not so sure about that.

We need the character we learn in good times as well as difficult times. Both have a different kind of value for us, and I don't think it's healthy to place one over the other, especially when it might lead us to develop habits of punishing ourselves unduly for the apparent promise of a later reward. Life doesn't always work that way; justice isn't necessarily the result of doing what we think is the right thing.

We also need care and kindness for their own sake. The acts of giving and receiving, and the quality of mercy and grace that these can embody, must be embedded within each step of the personal journey on which we seek to gain in character and achieve our purpose. And inviting others to be a part of our journey joins them to us and brings value to everyone – a shared journey gives us all that sense of belonging that we all need to become fully human.

So, to be kind is both a habit and a disposition. It's as much who we are as it is what we do. We don't have every aspect of life under our control. Cruel and unfair things happen to us, more often than we might expect. Sometimes, we need to be strong and defend ourselves with all of the armour we have. Maybe that's also one of the important reasons we also need both love and kindness. Our wounds need to be tended to and healed. Our faults need to be considered with understanding and forgiveness.

And sometimes we all just need a kind word or two.

> **REFLECTION: BE KIND**
>
> Being kind means consciously thinking of others, considering what they need to improve the experience of their lives and translating this into deliberate actions that support these needs.
>
> What acts of kindness do you perform on a regular basis?
>
> What else might you do?

Start with belonging

What does it mean to belong in your world? How might you welcome others into your world? How can you share your best gifts with them?

I believe that all of us need to know that we belong somewhere. That place and the people in it to whom we belong, in turn, need us to acknowledge their value to us through our courtesy, consideration and respect. This depends very much on our attitude. If we sit with each other and gnaw away at our individual and collective sense of worry, we will feed the apprehension of fear that can and most likely will kill off any genuine sense of belonging. We will end up turning inwards to fend for ourselves.

Instead, if we are generous with our gratitude and bold with our hope, we can and will achieve remarkable things for and with each other. In doing so, we will forge the bonds of trust that characterise an interdependence that speaks to a profound feeling of 'home'.

From the outset, in order for individuals to gain a genuine sense of 'home', they need to know that they are welcome and that they have a place where they feel as though others want them to be with them. They need the assurance that others (to use a phrase in common usage) 'have their back'. In time, the bonds that are formed through shared experiences of good times, bad times and ordinary times may come to form the kinship that can be called 'family', 'sisterhood' and 'brotherhood' (among other terms).

The biggest challenge to those seeking belonging is acceptance. Once a person has demonstrated that they qualify for a place, it must be granted by those who inhabit the space already. It is not possible to force one's way in, and, at the same time, one can't just stand by and wait to be accepted. There may be an exchange of kindnesses, which indicate a willingness to compromise one's own immediate needs in the interest of helping someone else by improving both their experience through the process and their outcomes through the product of collective relationship.

When someone feels as though they belong, they are much more likely to enter into the even closer ties of a relationship that can allow us to do more than just participate as one of many. This 'character apprenticeship' comes when an expert models, coaches and scaffolds us in the qualities of adaptive expertise and self-efficacy. They keep us in our groove and hold us to our purpose by inspiring, challenging and supporting us. We learn to articulate, reflect and explore. We gather and analyse evidence, make decisions and set goals.

We then need to learn how to work towards achieving our potential, whatever that may be. In time, we may even learn how to stretch the boundaries of our potential and expand our capacity, as well as come to understand the limitations and parameters within which we might sensibly aspire. Purpose, persistence and reflection are what will help us to lift our standard of performance. Our agency is shared between ourselves and the experts who will help us learn, and then let us go on to be experts in our own right.

People with strong civic and performance character are much more likely to seek to do that which is good and right in their life. They learn to shape for themselves a moral code and a set of ethics that act as the principles and structures by which they choose to live their lives. They acknowledge the influence and kindness of others and, in turn, seek to give back to others. Courage, honesty and humility make them both better at doing what they set out to do and better at creating a good impact on those around them. They become genuinely transformed and then support the transformation of their people and their place. They have come full circle – from seeking acceptance, they can act to provide acceptance and belonging. They can coach apprentices to achieve greater performance by realising potential.

In this way, as you grow in adaptive expertise and self-efficacy in **A Life of Purpose**, you can take on your own novices and teach them what you have learned. In the same way that others did this for you, you might hold up a mirror for them as they grow in competency so that they might see how they can belong, achieve their potential, and do good and right in the adventure of their lives.

In this book, I've mentioned some of the people in my life who have helped me to find my sense of purpose and realise it in how I learn, live, lead and work. I think what all of these people (and more besides who I am saving for the next three books) share in common with me is their capacity to express their love through their welcome. In the end, I am who I am, and I have done what I have done because they welcomed me into their lives. In doing so, they made their lives our shared life. They made and make me feel as though I belong. I wish the same for you in your life.

Reflection: Start with belonging

How do you recognise that others belong in your life?

How do you welcome them?

How do you pass on what you have learned to them?

How do you express your gratitude?

Step Forward and Up
Encounter

I believe that to prepare yourself to encounter the other properly in **A Life of Purpose**, you must first commit to a program of reflecting on who you have been, who you are and who you are becoming in the interdependence of the community with those around you. This ongoing, inside-out process of inquiry and transformation helps us to learn, live, lead and work through a life of purpose which is deeply imbued with the selflessness to put others before ourselves. It allows us to appreciate what my friend and colleague Adriano has taught me about the essence of encounter: that every person is home to a unique life.

With this in mind, let's review what we have learned in this final chapter. We have focused on five key ideas:

- ✓ Aim high
- ✓ Measure yourself and your impact
- ✓ Put others first
- ✓ Be kind
- ✓ Start with belonging

Think through each of these ideas again. Using what you learned in this chapter, review and revise your plan to help you to Step Forward and Up. Think through and write down answers to the following:

- **Plus** – What's one idea from this chapter that you could make happen in your life tomorrow? What could you do to make this happen? What help will you need? What's a really practical first thing that you could do to make this idea real in your life? What will you do to keep going? How will you know when it's making a difference?

- **Minus** – What's one idea from this chapter that doesn't seem right for you? Why isn't this idea right for you? Is it a case of 'not at all' or 'not yet'? How do you know whether you should hold your ground or shift your thinking on this idea?

- **Interesting** – What's one idea from this chapter that seems like it might be an interesting thing to do but which you're not yet ready to embrace? What might you need to do to ready yourself for this challenge? Who or what might help you to prepare you to take up this challenge in due course? How will you allow the time and space to do this preparation?

How would you like to Step Forward and Up from here? What will you add or subtract from your plan to make these new commitments work? Are you ready to form the plan as a whole and begin **A Life of Purpose**? Use these questions to prepare you to complete your plan:

- What excites you about the journey that lies ahead?
- What will you most need to make it happen?
- What will you most need others to do for you?

Just before you head off, I have one last set of ideas that might help you with **A Life of Purpose**. When you are ready, turn the page for the Conclusion.

Let's go!

Conclusion
Let's go!

In this first book of the **Character Education Series**, we have covered a lot of ground.

In travelling together on **A Life of Purpose**, I've shared with you what I've learned about how to identify and claim the fundamental reason why for your journey of exploration, discovery and encounter.

I've also invited you to Step Forward and Up in each of the three chapters by thinking through some questions and identifying three things that you can use to put into action your sense of what each of the elements of **A Life of Purpose** mean to you.

If you have found what we have done together to be valuable, then there are three further books in the series that you might like to consider:

- **The Pathway to Excellence** – how to learn, live, lead and work as you strive to become the best version of yourself.
- **Leading for Tomorrow's World** – how to connect your purpose to leadership which influences, inspires, directs and motivates others to build a shared vision for the future.

- **Make a Difference** – how to create a plan to put your sense of purpose into practice for the sake of people and place and planet.

Before we finish, there's one final thought I'd like to share with you…

Life is an adventure.

What will be your direction? Where will you go? How fast will you go? Where will you stop off on the way? How will you know when you get there?

Who will you take with you? What do you need to support you on the way? Who will you need for support?

Why will you do all of this?

The choices are yours to make. You have so many opportunities to make the most of your time here on Earth. You can achieve so much wherever you are if you have a compelling reason, a good plan and the right attitude to make it all happen.

I want you to come to know yourself, to earn your place, to go from me to you to us and to find your calling. I want you to grow in your expertise in relationship with others and to put your gifts and talents to their best use in our ever-changing world. I want you to learn from others, learn with others, do it yourself and then share what you have learned.

I want you to adopt a set of values that will hold you true to your course and select the right tools to tell your story of yesterday, today and tomorrow. I want you to have people who love and value you, and a place that feels like home. You'll also need a map to chart your way and some money in your pocket.

I want you to aspire to great things, and to locate that unique voice that enables you to express who you are and who you are becoming with confidence. I want you to grow strong and compassionate in your agency, and secure in your identity. I want you to learn to use the resources at your disposal wisely and to be well on every stage of your journey.

I want you to develop the character, competency and wellness to thrive in the world. I want you to feel as though you belong, that you are fulfilling your potential, and that you are doing good and right in the world. I want you to be able to tell your story of how you built the future by learning and unlearning what you needed, of how you designed solutions and created teams, of how you became a good person and a responsible citizen.

I don't want you to be alone as you travel. I want you to feel as though there is always a community with the right people to support, challenge and inspire you to become the person you need to be. I want you to have all of the right information you need to make better choices to learn, live, lead and work.

I want you to set off on your journey of exploration, discovery and encounter. I want you to enjoy your journey and claim your sense of purpose in the world.

I'm excited!

I can't wait!

Let's go!

www.ingramcontent.com/pod-product-compliance
Lightning Source LLC
Chambersburg PA
CBHW070335120526
44590CB00017B/2894